Christmas Goodies

By Esther Hautzig

Illustrated by Ronald Fritz

Random House 🏠 New York

Library of Congress Cataloging-in-Publication Data:
Hautzig, Esther Rudomin. Christmas goodies / by Esther Hautzig ; illustrated by Ronald Fritz. p. cm.
"Originally published in 1981 in somewhat different form"—T.p. verso. SUMMARY: A collection of simple recipes for Christmas candies, cookies, breads, cakes, and drinks. ISBN: 0-679-80133-2
1. Christmas cookery—Juvenile literature. [1. Christmas cookery] I. Fritz, Ronald, ill.
II. Title. TX739.2.C45H38 1989 641.5′68—dc19 88-43579

Manufactured in the United States of America   1 2 3 4 5 6 7 8 9 10

CONTENTS

GENERAL INSTRUCTIONS

Christmas is a time for special treats to share with friends and family. This book has festive recipes that are fun to make and delicious to eat. The recipes here also provide wonderful "I-made-it-especially-for-you" gifts. Allow enough time and follow these rules when you work in the kitchen. They will help you avoid accidents and ruined goodies. Make sure an adult is around to help you at all times.

Wash your hands before you start. Put on an apron or old short-sleeved T-shirt. Tie your hair, if it is long, so it won't get into your goodies. Read each recipe carefully. Gather all ingredients and utensils before you start. Measure all ingredients carefully.

Here are a few helpful hints:

- Remove paper wrappers from sticks of butter or margarine. Let butter or margarine reach room temperature before you use.
- When recipe calls for eggs, crack each one against the edge of a bowl and put it in separate bowl from the batter. Make sure that there are no bits of eggshell in

the egg. Then add the egg yolk and egg white to your batter. Put eggshells in garbage.

- To separate egg yolk from egg white, crack egg over a cup or small bowl. Let the white drip into bowl while you keep the egg yolk in the shell. If you only need egg white, put egg yolk into a small jar, pour a little milk over it, cover jar tightly, and refrigerate. Egg yolk can be used within a day or two. If you need only an egg yolk, store the egg white in a cup or small jar and refrigerate it for use also in a day or two.

- When recipe calls for nuts, use nuts that come already shelled and can be bought in cans or bags. It is difficult to shell nuts without getting bits of shell into your recipe.

- Use cookie sheets with raised edges. They are safer than entirely flat ones.

- To grease cookie sheet, cake pan, or loaf pan, put 1 tablespoon butter or margarine on a piece of clean paper towel or paper napkin. Grease the whole inside of the pan or cookie sheet. If 1 tablespoon isn't enough to thoroughly grease the pan or sheet, use more butter or margarine.

- When baking a large batch of cookies, regrease cookie sheet before putting new batch into oven. Wear oven mitts or use potholders if you grease sheet while it is hot.
- When recipe calls for buttered and floured cake pan, grease cake pan first. Then put a tablespoon or so of flour into greased pan and shake it so flour coats inside of pan. Shake out excess flour into garbage.
- Turn off electric mixer before you scrape down batter from sides of bowl (always use a rubber spatula to do this).

When you use electric appliances, such as a mixer or can opener, *always* ask for help from an adult. Plug in mixer only after all the moving parts are in. *Never* plug in electric appliances with wet hands! This can give you a painful shock. Unplug all appliances as soon as you are finished.

Always ask an adult to help you when you need a knife or other sharp utensils.

Most recipes in this book require you to use the stove or the oven. *Always* have an adult light the stove and oven for you and adjust the heat. Always use oven mitts or potholders when handling hot pots and pans. Always turn off the stove and oven when you are done.

Ask an adult to preheat the oven. This means to put oven on 15 minutes before you are ready to use it. Ask an adult if the temperature gauge on your stove works accurately. If it doesn't, your baked goodies may be either underbaked or burned. Most recipes, but not all, call for a preheated oven set to a particular temperature. Look into the oven once in a while to see how your cookies, candy, or cakes are doing. To test whether cake is done, ask an adult to insert a knife into middle of cake. If knife comes out dry, cake is done. Use oven mitts or potholders when you test the cake and handle a hot cake pan, and ask for help from an adult.

When you take a hot pot off the stove, use oven mitts or potholders and put the pot down on a heatproof surface. When you take a cookie sheet or cake pan out of the oven, use oven mitts or potholders and put sheet or pan on a cooling rack or on a heatproof surface.

Be careful! Always ask for help from an adult!
Use oven mitts or potholders! Don't rush! Have fun!

GOODIES FOR THE TREE

There are some recipes in this book, such as Candy Cookies, Gingerbread People, and Festive Christmas Tree Cookies, that can be hung from the branches of your tree as colorful ornaments.

When you prepare Gingerbread People and Festive Christmas Tree Cookies, ask an adult to help you make small holes in the tops of the cookies. One way to do this is for an adult to insert a toothpick in the top of the cookie before baking. Then bake the cookie with the toothpick still inserted. Once the cookie has cooled, remove the toothpick. A small hole will be in the top of the cookie. After the cookies are decorated, you can put colorful yarn through the holes for hanging the cookies.

Other things that look pretty on a Christmas tree are peppermint canes, lollipops tied with bright ribbons, and popcorn strings.

You can also hang other cookies and candies whose recipes are in this book. Wrap them in small pieces of clear plastic or colored cellophane, tie the "parcels" with pretty ribbons, and hang them on the tree. Take them down; remove the wrapping, yarn, or ribbon; and eat the goodies when you feel like it.

GIFT-WRAPPING YOUR GOODIES

If you plan to give away some of the goodies you make, wrap them nicely. Here are some ideas:

Save empty coffee cans, candy boxes, cookie tins and other tin boxes, egg cartons, glass jars with wide mouths, oatmeal cartons, and so on. Wash and dry glass jars and coffee cans. Shake out all tin boxes and cartons and line them with foil paper.

Decorate the outsides of the cans, boxes, cartons, and other containers with pretty pictures cut out from magazines or with shapes made out of self-adhesive paper. Egg cartons are especially good containers for candy. You can put candy into each egg compartment, and it will be well protected against breakage.

Use plastic bags if you do not have boxes, tins, or jars. Fill them with cookies, candies, or cakes and tie the bags with pretty ribbons.

You can decorate plain brown-paper bags with pictures from magazines or with crayon drawings, stars, or other ornamental stickers.

Wrap unfrosted cakes or breads in aluminum foil, and tie with ribbon.

If you are especially proud of your creation, copy the recipe on a pretty card or piece of paper and put it into your package.

Christmas Mints

Ingredients

3 egg whites
7 cups confectioners' sugar
Red and green food coloring
Mint extract

Utensils

Electric mixer and large
    mixing bowl
Measuring cup
2 bowls
Rubber spatula
Wax paper
Rolling pin
Small glass, doll teacup, or
    thimble
Metal spatula
Tray
Candy dish or box

Prepare this way

Put 3 egg whites into large mixing bowl. (To separate egg whites from egg yolks, see page 5.)

Ask an adult to help you now.

With electric mixer on high speed, beat egg whites. Add confectioners' sugar gradually as you beat, until mixture is very stiff.

Divide the mixture equally into two bowls. Use a few drops of red food coloring to tint the mixture in one bowl and a few drops of green food coloring to tint the mixture in the other bowl. Stir each mixture well with rubber spatula. (Wash spatula between mixing the two so that the colors don't get mixed up.) Put 3 or 4 drops of mint extract into each bowl. Mix each one well.

Put a piece of wax paper over a table. Put the mixture from one bowl on the wax paper. Cover with another piece of wax paper. With the rolling pin, roll the mixture between the pieces of wax paper until it is flat and about ¼ inch thick.

Take off top piece of wax paper. Cut out small mint patties with a very small glass, doll teacup, or thimble. Using metal spatula, put mint circles on a tray. Repeat with the other half of the candy mixture. Let the candy dry for about 8 hours. When all mints are dry, put them in candy dish or box. *Makes about 35 mints.*

Chocolate-Covered Fruits

Ingredients

A 12-ounce package
  semisweet chocolate
  morsels
1 tablespoon butter or
  margarine
1 teaspoon vanilla
1½ cups white raisins or
  dried figs, apricots, or
  dates

Utensils

Double boiler
Oven mitts or potholders
Long wooden mixing spoon
  and teaspoon
Cookie sheet
Paper towels
Measuring cup and spoons
Candy dish or box

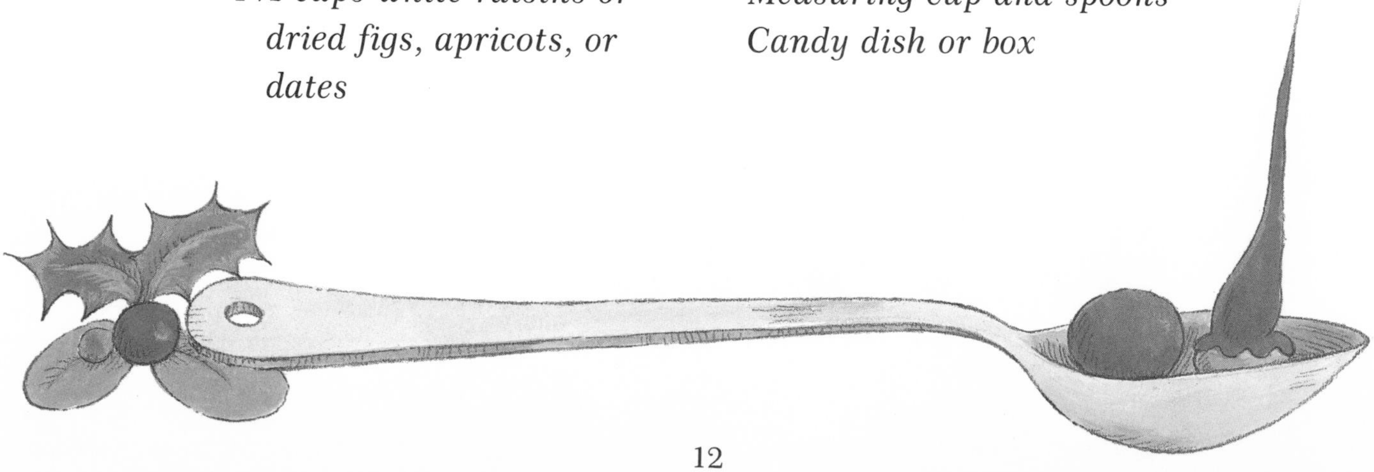

Prepare this way

Pour water into bottom part of double boiler until it's three-quarters full. Ask an adult to put pan on high flame on stove (see pages 6–7) and bring to a full boil. Using oven mitts or potholders, remove pot from stove.

Put chocolate morsels into top part of double boiler. Put it over the hot water in bottom part of double boiler. Be very careful when you do this. The pot is still very hot! Stir chocolate with mixing spoon until chocolate has melted. Add vanilla and mix.

Grease cookie sheet (see page 5).

If you are using raisins, put them all into the melted chocolate. Stir with mixing spoon until all raisins are coated. With teaspoon, take out small clusters of chocolate-covered raisins. Put each cluster on greased cookie sheet. Let the clusters cool and harden on cookie sheet in a cool part of your kitchen. (Do not refrigerate to speed hardening of chocolate, as it will lose its color.)

If you coat other fruits, such as dried figs, apricots, or dates, put a few at a time into melted chocolate. Stir well with mixing spoon to coat fruits. Remove one by one with teaspoon and put on greased cookie sheet to cool and harden at room temperature. Put in candy dish or box. *Makes about 1½ pounds of candy.*

Walnut Brittle

Ingredients

1 tablespoon butter or
    margarine
2 cups chopped walnuts
2 cups sugar
1 teaspoon vanilla

Utensils

Cookie sheet
Paper towels
Measuring cup and spoons
Heavy saucepan
Oven mitts or potholders
Long wooden mixing spoon
Candy dish or box

Prepare this way

Grease cookie sheet (see page 5).

Spread chopped walnuts evenly on the greased cookie sheet.

Put sugar into saucepan. Ask an adult to put saucepan over low flame on the stove (see pages 6–7). Using oven mitts or potholders, stir sugar with long mixing spoon until it melts and turns into a light brown syrup.

Still using oven mitts or potholders, take saucepan off stove. Put it on a heatproof surface. Add vanilla to the sugar syrup and stir well with wooden spoon.

Pour melted sugar slowly and evenly over nuts on cookie sheet. Ask an adult to help you do this. Let candy on cookie sheet cool until it is hard. Then break it into small pieces. Put into candy dish or box. *Makes about 1½ pounds of candy.*

Pecan-Caramel Candy

Ingredients

2 tablespoons butter or
   margarine, for greasing
   cookie sheet and spatula
2 cups pecan halves
A 14-ounce bag caramels

Utensils

Cookie sheet
Paper towels
Measuring cup
Oven mitts or potholders
Metal spatula
Wax paper
Candy dish or box

Prepare this way

Ask an adult to preheat oven to 325 degrees (see page 7).

Grease cookie sheet (see page 5). Put 4 or 5 pecan halves flat side down on cookie sheet in a flower-petal arrangement. Remove cellophane from caramels. Put a caramel candy in the center of each of the pecan flower groupings. Bake in oven for 5 to 6 minutes.

Using oven mitts or potholders, take cookie sheet out of oven. With a buttered metal spatula, flatten the caramel candy, which will be soft from being in the oven, until it spreads around and clings to the nuts. Cool on cookie sheet for about 5 minutes.

With the spatula, remove the candies from cookie sheet onto wax paper. Leave until completely cool. Then put in candy dish or box. *Makes about 1 pound of candy.*

Peppermint-Nut Candy

Ingredients

1½ cups vanilla cookie or
   gingersnap crumbs
1 cup crushed peppermint
   candies
6 tablespoons butter or
   margarine, plus 1
   tablespoon for greasing
   cookie sheet
1 cup chopped walnuts,
   pecans, or almonds

Utensils

Measuring cups
2 clean dishtowels and
   rolling pin
Bowl
Small saucepan or skillet
Oven mitts or potholders
Fork
Cookie sheet
Paper towels
Cooling rack
Candy dish or jar

Prepare this way

Ask an adult to preheat oven to 350 degrees (see page 7).

Prepare vanilla cookie or gingersnap crumbs. To do this, put cookies between two clean dishtowels and crush them with rolling pin.

Crush peppermint candies between two dishtowels with a rolling pin.

Put cookie crumbs and crushed peppermint candies into bowl.

Put 6 tablespoons butter into small saucepan or skillet and melt over very low flame. Have an adult help you. Wear oven mitts or use potholders when you handle saucepan or skillet. When butter or margarine has melted, remove from stove and add it to cookie-and-candy mixture in bowl. Mix well with fork.

Add nuts to the bowl and mix again.

Grease cookie sheet (see page 5). Spread candy-crumb-and-nut mixture on greased cookie sheet. Bake about 15 minutes. Using oven mitts or potholders, take cookie sheet out of the oven. Put on cooling rack and let candy cool completely. When cool, break into small pieces and put in candy dish or glass jar. Do not cover. *Makes about 1¼ pounds of candy.*

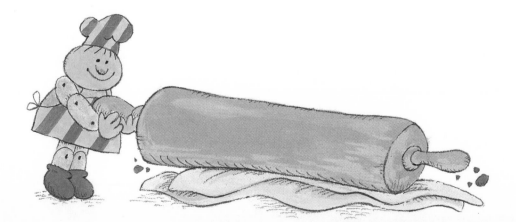

Coconut-Nut Candy

Ingredients

1¼ cups sugar

⅓ cup chopped walnuts,
  almonds, or pecans

1 cup flaked coconut

1 tablespoon butter or
  margarine

Utensils

Measuring cup

Heavy saucepan or skillet

Oven mitts or potholders

Long wooden mixing spoon

Cookie sheet

Paper towels

Cooling rack

Candy dish or box

Prepare this way

Put sugar into heavy saucepan or skillet. Have an adult put the pan over medium flame on the stove (see pages 6–7). Using oven mitts or potholders, stir constantly with long wooden spoon.

When sugar is melted and light brown in color, add the nuts and coconut. Again using oven mitts or potholders, stir a few times with long wooden spoon and remove pan from stove. Put on heatproof surface.

Grease cookie sheet (see page 5). Pour candy mixture over greased cookie sheet as evenly as you can. Have an adult help you with this. Use oven mitts or potholders.

Put cookie sheet on a rack and let the candy cool for at least 1 hour. When cool, break into small pieces and store in candy dish or box. *Makes about 1½ pounds of candy.*

Chocolate-Marshmallow Candy

Ingredients

1 package instant chocolate
    pudding
1 pound confectioners'
    sugar
1 egg white
2 tablespoons milk or cream
¾ stick butter or
    margarine
⅓ cup marshmallow cream
    (comes in jars)

Utensils

Large mixing bowl
Mixing spoon
Measuring cup and spoons
Cup
Small bowl
Large piece of wax paper
Rolling pin and board
Knife
Candy dish or box

Prepare this way

Put chocolate pudding powder into large mixing bowl. Add all but 4 tablespoons of confectioners' sugar to the pudding. Mix with mixing spoon.

Pour 2 tablespoons milk or cream over the sugar-and-pudding mixture.

Add 1 egg white. (To separate egg white from egg yolk, see page 5.) Mix the pudding and sugar with the milk and egg white.

Put ¾ stick butter or margarine into cup. Place cup in small bowl with hot tap water to soften the butter or margarine. Don't melt it entirely, just soften it a little. Ask an adult to help you with this.

Add the softened butter or margarine to the bowl with the pudding-and-sugar mixture. Mix it with the spoon for about 3 minutes. Then wash your hands well and dry them. Using your hands, mix the pudding-and-sugar mixture until it feels like dough. It will take about 3 or 4 minutes to do this.

Put the large piece of wax paper on the rolling board. Sprinkle 2 tablespoons confectioners' sugar on the wax paper and put the candy dough on top of it. With the rolling pin, roll out the candy dough until it is about ¼ inch thick. If the candy dough sticks to the rolling pin, sprinkle some confectioners' sugar on top of the dough. Try to roll it into a square shape, not a round one. Ask an adult to help you cut the dough into five strips, each 1½ inches wide.

Spread four of the strips with marshmallow cream and pile them on top of each other. Do not spread the fifth strip. Put it on top. Wrap the candy in the wax paper on which it was rolled and put it into the refrigerator for about 3 hours. Handle the candy carefully as you are putting it into the refrigerator so that you don't break it!

When the candy has hardened, take it out of the refrigerator and put it back on the rolling board. Open the wax-paper wrapping. Ask an adult to help you cut the candy strip into ¼-inch slices.

Put the candy on a pretty dish or in a candy box. Separate the layers of candy in candy box with wax paper so that they will not stick together. *Makes about 30 candies.*

Peanut Butter and Honey Balls

Ingredients

2 cups creamy peanut
    butter
2 cups honey
1 cup, approximately,
    powdered milk
Colored sprinkles

Utensils

Measuring cup and spoons
2 mixing bowls
Mixing spoon
Plate
Cookie sheet
Cookie jar or tin

Prepare this way

Put peanut butter and honey into a large bowl. Mix well with spoon.

Add enough powdered milk to the peanut butter and honey mixture to make it feel like dough. How much powdered milk you will need will depend on the consistency of your peanut-butter-and-honey mixture.

Wash your hands well. Put colored sprinkles onto a plate. Take a small piece of the mixture and form a ball. Roll each ball in colored sprinkles and place on cookie sheet.

When all the balls are made, put them in a cookie jar or tin. *Number of balls depends on size you make them.*

Stuffed Dates

Ingredients
1 box dates
1 cup, approximately,
   almonds or other nuts
Confectioners' sugar

Utensils
Knife
Bowl
Plate
Candy jar or tin or small
   serving plate

Prepare this way

Make sure all dates are pitted. If they aren't, have an adult help you remove the pits with a knife. Stuff an almond, or other nut, into each date. Place all stuffed dates in a bowl.

Pour some confectioners' sugar on a plate. Roll each stuffed date in the confectioners' sugar, shake off excess, and store in a jar or tin, or serve immediately on a pretty plate. *Makes as many dates as there are in the box.*

Christmas Tree Cookies

Ingredients

2 sticks butter or margarine, plus 1 tablespoon for greasing cookie sheet

1 cup sugar

1 egg

1 teaspoon vanilla

2¼ cups flour, plus 2 tablespoons for flouring rolling board and pin

½ teaspoon baking powder

Colored sugar, candied cherries, citron, chocolate morsels, gumdrops, red-hots, etc., and tubes of ready-made icing

Utensils

Electric mixer and large mixing bowl

Measuring cup and spoons

Sifter

Rubber spatula

Rolling pin and board

Cookie cutters

Cookie sheet

Paper towels

Metal spatula

Oven mitts or potholders

Cooling rack

Cookie jar or tin

Yarn or thread

Prepare this way

Put 2 sticks of butter and the sugar into large mixing bowl.

With electric mixer set on medium speed, beat until light and fluffy. Ask an adult to help you.

Add the egg and vanilla and continue mixing.

Gradually sift flour and baking powder directly into bowl with batter. Mix with rubber spatula. As dough gets thicker, mix it with your hands. (Make sure your hands are clean!) When well mixed, chill dough in the refrigerator for 2 hours.

Ask an adult to preheat oven to 350 degrees (see page 7).

Take dough out of the refrigerator. Sprinkle flour lightly on rolling board and rolling pin. Roll out half the dough to thickness of about ¼ inch. Cut out pretty shapes with whatever cookie cutters you have.

Grease cookie sheet (see page 5). Using metal spatula, transfer cookies from board to cookie sheet. Put them about 1 inch apart. If you plan to hang cookies from your tree, see page 8. Bake about 10 minutes. While the cookies bake, roll out the rest of the dough, and cut it into shapes you like.

Using oven mitts or potholders, take cookie sheet out of the oven. Transfer cookies to cooling rack, using metal spatula. Grease cookie sheet again (remember it will still be hot, so use oven mitts or potholders) and bake the second batch.

When all cookies are done and well cooled, decorate them with colorful icing from tubes, and with all the other fruits and candies you have assembled. Make tree-shaped cookies look like miniature Christmas trees, give the birds colorful plumes, and so on. Store cookies in large cookie jar or tin. Just before you hang them on your tree, pull yarn or thread through holes on top and make loops. *Makes about 35 cookies, depending on shape and size.*

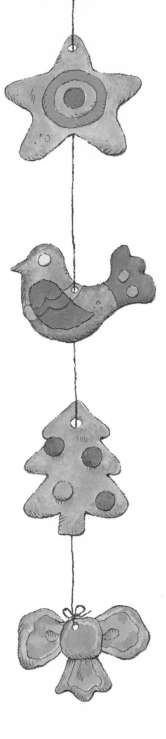

Chocolate Chip – Raisin Cookies

Ingredients

2 sticks butter or
   margarine
1 cup brown sugar
½ cup white sugar
1 egg
1 teaspoon vanilla
2 cups flour
1 teaspoon baking soda
A 12-ounce package
   semisweet chocolate
   morsels
1 cup raisins

Utensils

Electric mixer and large
   mixing bowl
Measuring cup and spoons
Sifter
Rubber spatula
Cookie sheet
Oven mitts or potholders
Cooling rack
Metal spatula
Cookie jar or tin

Prepare this way

Have an adult preheat oven to 350 degrees (see page 7).

Put butter or margarine into large mixing bowl. Add the brown sugar and white sugar. With electric mixer set on medium speed, beat until light and fluffy. Ask an adult to help you.

Add egg and vanilla to batter and continue beating until well mixed.

Sift flour and baking soda directly into bowl with batter. Mix flour into batter with a rubber spatula. Add the chocolate morsels and raisins. Mix again with rubber spatula until everything is well blended.

Form little balls of batter with your hands. Put them about 2 inches apart on an ungreased cookie sheet. Bake about 15 minutes. Using oven mitts or potholders, take cookie sheet out of oven. Set it on cooling rack. Let cookies cool directly on the cookie sheet. When cool, remove cookies with metal spatula and put into airtight cookie jar or tin. Repeat, baking more batches, until all batter has been used. *Makes about 60 cookies*.

Orange Drop Cookies

Ingredients

1 stick butter or margarine,
  plus 1 tablespoon for
  greasing cookie sheet
1¼ cups sugar
1 cup sour cream
⅓ cup orange juice
2¼ cups flour
1 teaspoon baking soda
½ teaspoon cinnamon
Tubes of ready-made icing
Candied citron or colored
  sugar

Utensils

Measuring cup and spoons
Electric mixer and large
  mixing bowl
Sifter
Rubber spatula
Cookie sheet
Paper towels
Teaspoons
Oven mitts or potholders
Cooling rack
Metal spatula
Cookie jar or tin

Prepare this way

Have an adult preheat oven to 350 degrees (see page 7).

Put 1 stick butter or margarine and sugar into large mixing bowl. With electric mixer set on medium speed, beat until light and fluffy. Ask an adult to help you.

Add the sour cream and orange juice and beat again until well mixed.

Sift flour, baking soda, and cinnamon directly into bowl. Mix well with rubber spatula. Grease cookie sheet (see page 5). Drop teaspoonfuls of dough onto the cookie sheet about 2 inches apart. Cookies will spread and need the room. Bake for 15 minutes.

Using oven mitts or potholders, put cookie sheet on cooling rack. When cookies are completely cool, remove them from cookie sheet with metal spatula. Decorate them with icing from tubes. Put pieces of candied citron, or sprinkle colored sugar, over icing. Store in cookie jar or tin. *Makes about 50 cookies*.

Gingerbread People

Ingredients

2 sticks butter or
    margarine, plus 1
    tablespoon for greasing
    cookie sheet
1 cup sugar
1 egg
1 cup molasses
2 tablespoons white vinegar
5 cups flour, plus 2
    tablespoons for flouring
    rolling board and rolling
    pin
1½ teaspoons baking soda
2½ teaspoons ginger
1 teaspoon cinnamon
½ teaspoon ground cloves
Red-hots, raisins, tubes of
    ready-made icing

Utensils

Measuring cup and spoons
Electric mixer and large
    mixing bowl
Sifter
Bowl
Rubber spatula
Rolling pin and board
Gingerbread-people cookie
    cutter
Cookie sheet
Paper towels
Metal spatula
Oven mitts or potholders
Cooling rack
Cookie jar or tin
Yarn or thread

Prepare this way

Put the butter or margarine and the sugar into large mixing bowl. With electric mixer set on medium speed, beat until well blended. Add egg, molasses, and vinegar. Beat again until well blended. Ask an adult to help you use the mixer.

Sift flour, baking soda, ginger, cinnamon, and ground cloves into separate bowl. Gradually add this sifted flour-and-spices mixture into bowl with batter. Mix with rubber spatula. As dough gets thicker, mix it with your hands. (Make sure your hands are clean!) When well mixed, chill dough in the refrigerator for 2 hours.

Have an adult preheat oven to 375 degrees (see page 7).

Take dough out of the refrigerator. Sprinkle flour lightly on rolling board and rolling pin. Roll out one quarter of the dough to a thickness of about ⅛ inch. Cut out gingerbread people with cookie cutter. If you have other cookie cutters, such as Christmas trees, you can use them too.

Grease cookie sheet (see page 5). Using metal spatula, transfer gingerbread people from rolling board to cookie sheet. Put them about 1 inch apart.

If you plan to hang gingerbread people from your Christmas tree, see page 8.

Bake for 6–8 minutes.

Using oven mitts or potholders, take cookie sheet out of the oven. Transfer cookies carefully from cookie sheet to cooling rack, using metal spatula.

Roll out more dough and cut out more gingerbread people. Grease cookie sheet again, using oven mitts or potholders. Cookie sheet will still be very hot! Repeat baking, transferring cookies to cooling rack, and so on, until all are done!

When all the gingerbread people are ready and cool, decorate them with icing from tubes. Make hair, outline costumes, and so on. Use red-hots for buttons and raisins for eyes and mouths.

Store cookies in cookie jar or tin. Just before you hang your cookies on a Christmas tree, pull yarn or thread through holes on top and make loops. *Makes about 50 cookies, depending on size and shape.*

Candy Cookies

This is the most difficult recipe in the book because it takes skill to peel off the wax paper from the baked cookies. Have an adult help you. Follow instructions and work slowly and carefully.

Ingredients
⅓ cup butter or margarine
⅓ cup sugar
1 egg
⅔ cup honey
1 teaspoon almond extract
3 cups flour
1 teaspoon baking soda
Sourballs, lollipops, or other hard, colorful candies, crushed into bits

Utensils
Measuring cup and spoons
Electric mixer and large mixing bowl
Sifter
2 bowls
Rubber spatula
2 clean dishtowels
Rolling pin and board
Wax paper
Cookie sheet
Oven mitts or potholders
Cooling rack
Cookie jar or tin
Yarn or ribbon

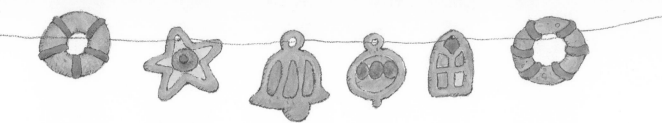

Prepare this way

Put butter or margarine, sugar, egg, honey, and almond extract into large mixing bowl. With electric mixer set on medium speed, beat until well blended. Ask an adult to help you.

Sift flour and baking soda into separate bowl. Gradually add flour mixture to batter in large mixing bowl. Mix with rubber spatula. As dough gets thicker, use your hands. (Make sure your hands are clean!) When dough is well mixed, refrigerate for 2 hours.

Crush sourballs, lollipops, or other hard candy between two clean dishtowels. Use a rolling pin, mallet, or hammer. Put crushed candy into small bowl.

Have an adult preheat oven to 375 degrees (see page 7).

Take dough out of the refrigerator. Sprinkle flour lightly on rolling board. Using the palms of your hands, roll dough into thin strips. Put a piece of wax paper over cookie sheet. Arrange strips of dough in open designs, such as flowers, butterflies, pendants, or others shown on these pages. Leave open space in the designs to be filled in with crushed candy, and a small hole where yarn or ribbon can be threaded for hanging cookies on your tree.

Bake in oven for about 5 minutes. Using oven mitts or potholders, take cookie sheet from the oven and set it on cooling rack. Fill the open areas of your designs with a thin layer of crushed candies. (Remember to leave one part of the design open for pulling through the yarn or ribbon.) Bake again for 3 minutes. Watch carefully that the cookies don't burn and that the candy colors do not become dull and very dark.

Again, using oven mitts or potholders, take the cookie sheet out of the oven and set it on a rack to cool. When the cookie sheet is cool and cookies are easy to handle, peel off the wax paper from the backs of the cookies. This is extremely difficult. Ask an adult to help you.

Store cookies in an airtight cookie jar or tin until you are ready to hang them on your tree. Then pull pieces of yarn or ribbon through the empty spaces you left in your designs.

These are rather tricky, but very lovely, ornamental cookies and worth the trouble it takes to make them. However, you can also roll out the dough, cut it into various shapes, and bake it without the candies, then hang it on your tree or store in a cookie jar or tin. *The number of cookies will depend on how you "design" them, and how big you make them.*

Your-Own-Initial
Butter Cookies

Ingredients

1 stick butter or margarine,
 plus 1 tablespoon for
 greasing cookie sheet
½ cup sugar
2 egg yolks
3 tablespoons milk
1½ cups flour, plus 1 or 2
 tablespoons for flouring
 rolling board
2 egg whites
Cinnamon sugar

Utensils

Measuring cup and spoons
Electric mixer and large
 mixing bowl
2 bowls
Sifter
Rubber spatula
Rolling pin and board
Fork or whisk
Pastry brush
Cookie sheet
Paper towels
Metal spatula
Oven mitts or potholders
Cooling rack
Cookie jar or tin

YUM·YUM

Prepare this way

Put 1 stick butter or margarine and sugar into large mixing bowl. With electric mixer set on medium speed, beat until light and fluffy. Ask an adult to help you.

Separate egg yolks from egg whites (see page 5). Save the whites. Add the egg yolks and milk to the large bowl and beat until well mixed.

Sift 1½ cups flour a little at a time directly into bowl with batter. Mix with rubber spatula. As dough gets thicker, mix with hands until all the flour has been blended into batter. Chill in the refrigerator for 1 to 2 hours.

Have an adult preheat oven to 325 degrees (see page 7).

Take dough out of the refrigerator. Sprinkle 1 or 2 tablespoons flour lightly on rolling board. Roll out thin ropes of dough and shape them into your initials or initials of your friends or relatives. You can make them any size!

Beat egg white with a fork or whisk. Brush the cookies with the beaten egg white, using a pastry brush. Sprinkle with cinnamon sugar.

Grease cookie sheet (see page 5). Using metal spatula, transfer initial cookies from rolling board to cookie sheet. Bake for about 10–12 minutes.

Using oven mitts or potholders, take cookie sheet out of the oven. Cool on cooling rack. Take cookies off cookie sheet with metal spatula and put in cookie jar or tin with tight cover. *Makes 30 to 35 cookies, depending on size.*

Ice Cream Pie

Ingredients

1 cup graham cracker
  crumbs

1 tablespoon sugar

½ stick butter or
  margarine

1 package strawberry
  gelatin

1 cup hot tap water

1 pint strawberry or vanilla
  ice cream

½ cup heavy cream

1 tablespoon confectioners'
  sugar

Colored sprinkles

Utensils

Measuring cup and spoons

2 mixing bowls; 1 small
  bowl

2 clean dishtowels and
  rolling pin

Cup

Mixing spoon

9-inch deep-dish pie pan

Electric mixer and large
  mixing bowl

Aluminum foil

Prepare this way

To make cookie crumbs, put graham crackers between two clean dishtowels and crush with rolling pin. Put 1 cup graham cracker crumbs into small bowl. Add 1 tablespoon sugar to the crumbs. Mix with spoon.

Put ½ stick butter or margarine into cup. Melt the butter or margarine by placing cup into bowl with hot tap water. Ask an adult to help you with this.

Add the melted butter or margarine to the crumbs. Mix together well with spoon.

Line the bottom and sides of the pie pan with the graham cracker mixture. Wash your hands well and dry them. With your fingers, press the graham cracker mixture to the inside of the pan.

Put the strawberry gelatin powder into large mixing bowl. Add 1 cup hot tap water. Stir with mixing spoon.

Add 1 pint strawberry or vanilla ice cream to the gelatin and water. Stir again with spoon until ice cream has melted. Let the mixture stand for 5 minutes. Then beat the ice-cream-and-gelatin mixture with the electric mixer for 5 minutes, so that it becomes light and fluffy. Ask an adult to help you use the electric mixer.

Spoon the ice-cream-and-gelatin mixture into the pie pan lined with graham cracker crumbs. Cover with aluminum foil and put in the refrigerator for at least 4 hours before serving.

Just before you serve the pie, ask an adult to help you whip ½ cup heavy cream with 1 tablespoon confectioners' sugar until the cream is stiff. Spread the whipped cream on top of the pie and put colored sprinkles over the cream. *Serves 8*.

Christmas Cherry Pie

Ingredients

A 16-ounce can of pitted
  cherries, in light or heavy
  syrup
1 cup lemon-snap cookie
  crumbs
½ stick butter or
  margarine
1 package instant vanilla
  pudding
1¼ cups milk
Chocolate or colored
  sprinkles or Christmas
  candies

Utensils

Measuring cup and spoons
Sieve
Can opener
1 large bowl; 1 small bowl
2 clean dishtowels and
  rolling pin
Cup
Electric mixer and large
  mixing bowl
9-inch deep-dish pie pan
Wax paper

Prepare this way

Have an adult open the can of cherries. Over the sink, pour the cherries into the sieve. Shake the sieve to drain off all the syrup.

44

To make cookie crumbs, put lemon snaps between two clean dishtowels and crush with rolling pin. Put 1 cup lemon-snap cookie crumbs into small bowl.

Put ½ stick butter or margarine into cup. Melt it by placing cup into bowl with hot tap water. Ask an adult to help you with this.

Add the melted butter or margarine to the cookie crumbs. Mix together well with spoon.

Line the bottom and sides of the pie pan with the cookie-crumb mixture. Wash your hands well and dry them. With your fingers, press the cookie-crumb mixture to the inside of the pan.

Open the package of vanilla pudding mix and put the pudding powder into large mixing bowl. Slowly add 1¼ cups milk. Mix the pudding powder and the milk with the electric mixer. Ask an adult to help you with this. Mix until the mixture is smooth.

Put the cherries on top of the cookie-crumb crust. Save a few of the cherries to decorate the top of the pie. Put the pudding mixture over cherries and crust. Cover with wax paper. Put into refrigerator to chill for 3 hours.

Before serving pie, decorate the top with cherries you have saved, colored sprinkles, or Christmas candies. *Serves 8*.

Banana Bread

Ingredients

¼ cup sour cream
1 teaspoon baking soda
3 ripe bananas or enough
   to equal 1 cup mashed
1 stick butter or margarine,
   plus 1 tablespoon for
   greasing loaf pan
1¼ cups sugar
2 eggs
1 teaspoon vanilla
1½ cups flour, plus 1
   tablespoon for flouring
   loaf pan

Utensils

Measuring cup and spoons
2 bowls
Fork
Electric mixer and large
   mixing bowl
Rubber spatula
Loaf pan
Paper towels
Oven mitts or potholders
Cooling rack

Prepare this way

Have an adult preheat oven to 350 degrees (see page 7).

Mix sour cream and baking soda in small bowl. Sour cream will rise as it stands in bowl.

In another bowl, mash 3 peeled ripe bananas with fork.

Put 1 stick butter or margarine into large mixing bowl. With electric mixer set on medium speed, beat while you add the sugar. Continue beating until fluffy. Add eggs and vanilla and continue beating until well mixed. Ask an adult to help you.

Add flour alternately with mashed bananas to the batter, using electric mixer set at the lowest speed. Add sour cream and mix it in with rubber spatula.

Grease and flour loaf pan (see page 6). Spoon batter into pan and bake for about 50 minutes. Using oven mitts or potholders, take pan out of the oven. Put on cooling rack for about 2 hours. *Serves 10 to 12.*

Orange-Nut Bread

Ingredients

1 stick butter or margarine,
  plus 1 tablespoon for
  greasing cake pan

½ cup sugar

2 eggs

2 cups whole-wheat flour

2½ teaspoons baking
  powder

½ cup honey

½ cup orange juice

1½ cups chopped walnuts
  or pecans

Utensils

Electric mixer and large
  mixing bowl

Measuring cup and spoons

Sifter

2 bowls

Rubber spatula

Loaf pan

Paper towels

Oven mitts or potholders

Cooling rack

Prepare this way

Have an adult preheat oven to 350 degrees (see page 7).

Put 1 stick butter or margarine into large mixing bowl. With electric mixer set on medium speed, beat while you add the sugar. Continue beating until fluffy. Ask an adult to help you.

Add eggs, one at a time, while you continue beating.

Sift flour and baking powder into separate bowl. Combine the honey and orange juice in another bowl. Add the flour alternately with the juice-and-honey mixture to batter in mixing bowl. Use electric mixer set at the lowest speed until everything is well blended.

Add chopped nuts to the batter. Stir well with rubber spatula.

Grease loaf pan (see page 5). Spoon batter into pan and smooth top with spatula. Bake for about 50 minutes. Using oven mitts or potholders, take cake pan out of the oven and cool on rack for about 1 hour. *Serves 10 to 12.*

Christmas Fruit-and-Nut Cake

Ingredients

2 sticks butter or margarine, plus 1 tablespoon for greasing cake pan

1½ cups sugar, plus ¼ cup sugar for fruits and nuts

3 eggs

1 teaspoon vanilla

3½ cups flour, plus ¼ cup flour for fruits and nuts

3 teaspoons baking powder

⅓ cup water

1 cup chopped candied fruits

½ cup chopped walnuts or pecans or almonds

Utensils

Electric mixer and large mixing bowl

Measuring cup and spoons

Sifter

2 bowls

Rubber spatula

10-inch tube pan

Paper towels

Oven mitts or potholders

Cooling rack

Metal spatula or knife

Cake plate

Prepare this way

Have an adult preheat oven to 350 degrees (see page 7).

Put 2 sticks butter or margarine into large mixing bowl. Add 1½ cups sugar. With electric mixer set on medium speed, beat until light and fluffy. Ask an adult to help you.

Add eggs, one at a time, and continue beating. Add vanilla and beat again.

Sift 3½ cups of flour and baking soda into separate bowl. Add the flour mixture and ⅓ cup water, a little at a time, to the batter in the mixing bowl, using electric mixer set at the lowest speed. Stop mixing when batter is well blended.

Put candied fruits and nuts into another bowl. Sprinkle them with ¼ cup flour and ¼ cup sugar. Using rubber spatula, stir the fruits and nuts with the flour and sugar until well mixed. Add them to batter. Mix the batter with a rubber spatula until well blended.

Grease the tube pan (see page 5). Put batter into tube pan and smooth the top with rubber spatula.

Bake for about 60 minutes. Using oven mitts or potholders, take pan out of the oven. Put on cooling rack for about 1½ hours. When cake is cool, loosen the edges with metal spatula or knife. Put cake plate over pan and ask an adult to turn plate and pan upside down. *Serves 12 to 15.*

Christmas Tree Cake

Ingredients

¾ cup sugar

1¼ cups flour

1½ teaspoons baking powder

¾ cup milk

1 teaspoon vanilla

½ stick butter or margarine, plus 1 tablespoon for greasing pan

1 egg

A 16½-ounce can of ready-made white icing

Green food coloring

Gumdrops, red-hots, colored sugar, silver balls, M&M's, raisins, miniature marshmallows, chocolate morsels, etc.

Utensils

Measuring cup and spoons

Sifter

Electric mixer and large mixing bowl

Rubber spatula

9-inch-square baking pan

Paper towels

Oven mitts or potholders

Cooling rack

Can opener

Cutting board

Knife

Cake platter

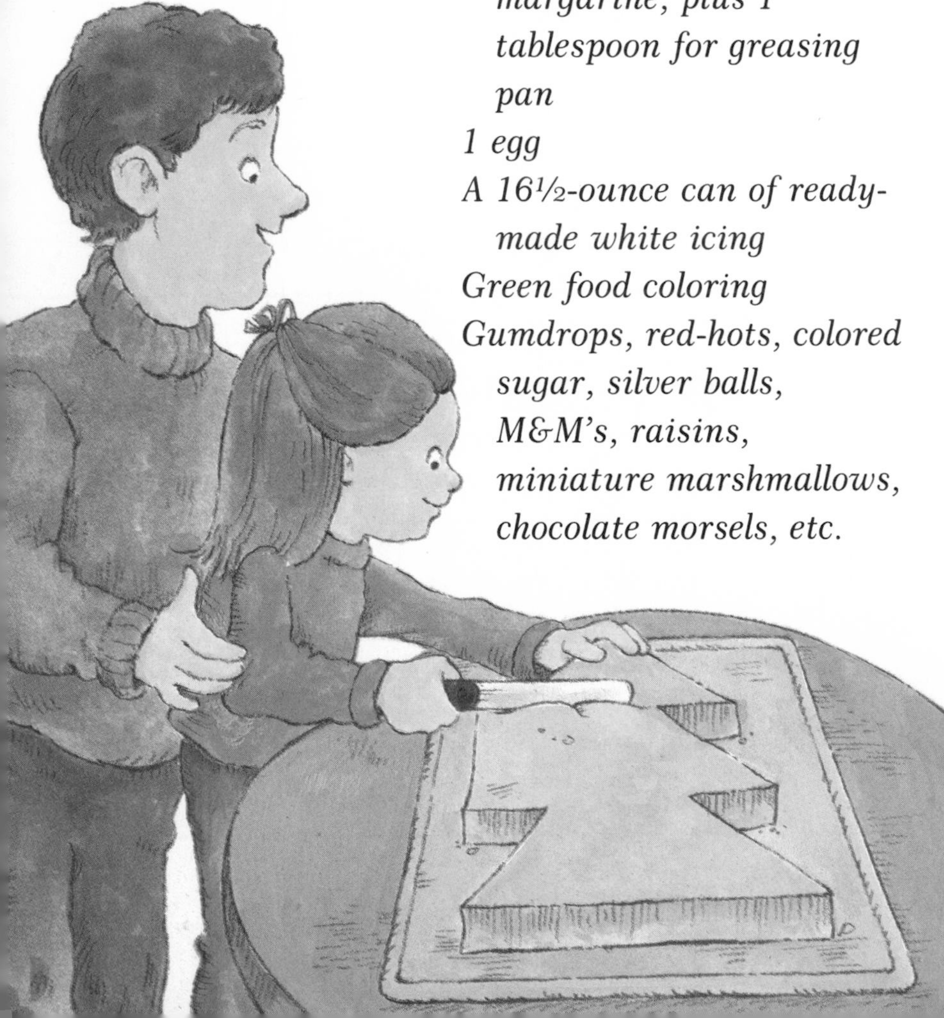

Prepare this way

Have an adult preheat oven to 350 degrees (see page 7).

Sift sugar, flour, and baking powder into large mixing bowl. Add milk and vanilla. Mix with rubber spatula.

Add ½ stick butter or margarine and the egg. With electric mixer set at low speed, beat for 3 minutes. Ask an adult to help you. Stop mixer. Scrape down the dough from the sides of bowl, using rubber spatula. Beat again for 5 minutes on high speed.

Grease the baking pan (see page 6). Spoon batter into baking pan and bake for 40 minutes. Using oven mitts or potholders, take cake pan out of the oven. Cool on cooling rack for at least 1 hour.

Open the can of white cake icing. Put a few drops of green food coloring into it. Mix with spoon so it is a nice Christmas-tree green.

When cake is cool, loosen the edges with metal spatula or knife. Place cutting board over pan and ask an adult to turn board and cake upside down. Cut the cake into shape shown in the illustration on opposite page. Put the Christmas-tree-shaped cake on cake platter. Ice with green icing and a variety of candies, gumdrops, red-hots, colored sugar, silver balls, M&M's, raisins, miniature marshmallows, chocolate morsels, and so on. *Serves 8*.

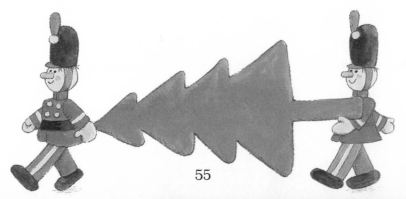

Very Easy Chocolate Cake

Ingredients

1½ cups flour
1 cup sugar
1 teaspoon baking soda
3 tablespoons cocoa
6 tablespoons oil
1 tablespoon white vinegar
1 teaspoon vanilla
1 cup cold water
A 16½-ounce can of ready-made icing
Gumdrops, red-hots, M&M's, colored sugar, silver balls, etc.

Utensils

Measuring cup and spoons
Sifter
8-inch-square cake pan
Small spoon
Small metal spatula
Mixing fork
Oven mitts or potholders
Cooling rack
Can opener

Prepare this way

Have an adult preheat oven to 350 degrees (see page 7).

Sift flour, sugar, baking soda, and cocoa directly into ungreased cake pan.

Using small spoon or metal spatula, make three holes or wells in the mixture. Pour oil into first hole, vinegar into second hole, and vanilla into third hole.

Pour 1 cup cold water over all the ingredients. Stir mixture with a fork until it is all well blended. Bake for 35 minutes. Using oven mitts or potholders, take pan out of the oven. Put on cooling rack.

When cake is completely cool, decorate it with ready-made icing from a can (ask an adult to open can for you) and with gumdrops, red-hots, M&M's, colored sugar, silver balls, or any combination of these goodies. Cut pieces of cake with spatula and serve directly from the pan. *Serves 8*.

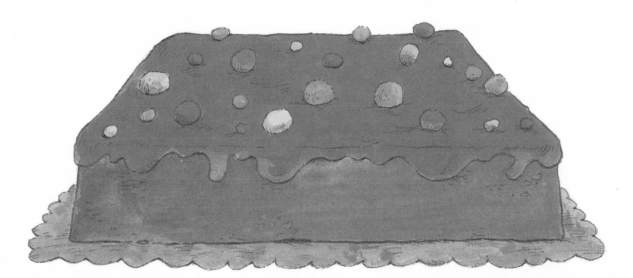

Cherry-Cheese Tarts

Ingredients

¾ cup cookie crumbs

An 8-ounce package of
   cream cheese

⅓ cup sugar

1 teaspoon lemon juice

1 teaspoon vanilla

1 egg

A 20-ounce can of cherry
   pie filling

Utensils

Muffin baking pan and
   paper muffin cups

Measuring cup and spoons

2 clean dishtowels and
   rolling pin

Electric mixer and large
   mixing bowl

Oven mitts or potholders

Cooling rack

Platter or tray

Can opener

Prepare this way

Have an adult preheat oven to 375 degrees (see page 7).

To make cookie crumbs, put cookies between two clean dishtowels and crush them with a rolling pin. Vanilla cookies and gingersnaps work the best.

Line the muffin baking pan with paper muffin cups. Put about 1 tablespoon of cookie crumbs into each muffin cup. Put cream cheese, sugar, lemon juice, and vanilla into large mixing bowl. With electric mixer set on medium speed, beat for about 3 minutes. Add egg and continue beating for another 2 minutes. Ask an adult to help you.

Put about 2 tablespoons of the cheese mixture into each of the muffin cups, over the cookie crumbs. Put baking pan into oven and bake for 15 minutes. Using oven mitts or potholders, take the baking pan out of the oven. Put on cooling rack and let cool for about 1 hour.

Take the paper muffin cups out of the baking pan. Put them on a tray or platter. Ask an adult to open can of cherry pie filling. Put about 2 tablespoons of cherry pie filling over the cheese in each of the muffin cups. Refrigerate for an hour or more, and serve. *Makes 12 tarts.*

Christmas Punch

Ingredients

¾ cup orange juice

¼ cup lemon juice

1 cup strong tea

½ cup sugar

1 quart ginger ale

1 quart club soda

A 6- or 8-ounce can
  mandarin orange sections

Decorative ice cubes (see
  recipe, page 63)

Utensils

Measuring cup

1-quart, or larger, pitcher
  or bottle

Long mixing spoon

Can opener

Punch bowl and ladle

Punch cups or tall glasses

Prepare this way

Pour orange juice, lemon juice, tea, and sugar into bottle or pitcher. Stir these ingredients. Refrigerate at least 2 hours. Also refrigerate the ginger ale and club soda.

Ask an adult to open the can of mandarin oranges when you are ready to serve punch. Pour contents of can into punch bowl. Add the juice-and-tea mixture to the bowl. Stir well.

Add the chilled ginger ale, club soda, and decorative ice cubes. Serve in punch cups or tall glasses. *Serves 8.*

Warm Cranberry Punch

Ingredients

1 quart cranberry juice
2 cups orange juice
¼ cup honey
1 cinnamon stick
5 whole cloves
1 quart bottle lemon-lime
  soda

Utensils

Large saucepan
Mixing spoon
Oven mitts or potholders
Trivet
Strainer
Punch bowl and ladle
Punch cups

Prepare this way

Pour cranberry juice, orange juice, and honey into large saucepan. Add cinnamon stick and cloves.

Have an adult put saucepan over low flame (see pages 6–7). Simmer the juice for about 15 minutes. Stir a few times with mixing spoon.

Using oven mitts or potholders, take saucepan off the stove. Put it on a trivet or on a heatproof surface. Let the punch cool for about 15 minutes.

Put strainer over punch bowl. Pour punch slowly into bowl through the strainer. Discard the cloves and cinnamon stick. Add 1 quart lemon-lime soda at room temperature to the punch. Serve in punch cups while still warm, but not hot. *Serves 12.*

Warm Cider

Ingredients

½ gallon sweet apple cider
2 sticks of cinnamon
8 cloves
1 unpeeled orange
5 whole allspice

Utensils

Large saucepan
Mixing spoon
Oven mitts or potholders
Trivet
Strainer
Punch bowl and ladle
Punch cups

Prepare this way

Pour apple cider into large saucepan. Add cinnamon sticks. Stick cloves into unpeeled orange. Add the clove-studded orange and the allspice to cider.

Have an adult put saucepan over low flame (see pages 6–7). Simmer the cider for about 20 minutes. Stir a few times with mixing spoon.

Using oven mitts or potholders, take saucepan off the stove. Put it on a trivet or on a heatproof surface. Let the cider cool for 15 minutes.

Put strainer over punch bowl. Pour cider slowly into bowl through the strainer. Discard the orange, allspice, and cinnamon sticks. Serve in punch cups while still warm, but not hot. *Serves 8*.

Decorative
Ice Cubes or Ring

Ingredients
1 small can pineapple
   chunks or 1 small can
   mandarin orange sections

Utensils
Can opener
Small strainer
Measuring cup
Ice tray or small round
   gelatin mold

Prepare this way

Have an adult open small can of pineapple chunks or mandarin orange sections. Put small strainer over measuring cup. Pour the syrup from can into cup. Add cold water to fill the cup.

Pour the syrup and water into ice tray until three-quarters full. Put into each ice-cube compartment a mandarin section or pineapple chunk. Freeze.

If you serve punch and need to keep it chilled in a punch bowl, make a decorative ice ring. It won't melt as quickly as ice cubes and will keep your punch cold for a longer time. To make it, pour the syrup and pineapple chunks or the syrup and mandarin sections directly into gelatin mold. Add enough cold water to fill the mold three-quarters full. Freeze.

Christmas Relish

Ingredients

1 large can whole cranberry
 sauce
1 seedless orange
½ cup raisins
½ cup chopped almonds or
 walnuts

Utensils

Can opener
Large mixing bowl
Mixing spoon
Knife
Measuring cup
Bowl or jar

Prepare this way

Have an adult open the can of whole cranberry sauce. Put the sauce into large mixing bowl. Mix with spoon.

Peel orange and remove all the white pith that you can. Ask an adult to help you use the knife to cut the orange sections into small pieces. Add pieces to the cranberry sauce in bowl.

Add ½ cup raisins and ½ cup chopped almonds or walnuts to the cranberry-and-orange mixture. Mix well with spoon.

Put into pretty serving bowl or jar and chill in the refrigerator for at least an hour before serving. *Serves 6 to 8.*